Writing
A PHILOSOPHY STATEMENT
An Educator's Workbook

caroline pryor

Texas A&M University

McGraw Hill **Custom Publishing**

Boston   Burr Ridge, IL   Dubuque, IA   Madison, WI   New York
San Francisco   St. Louis   Bangkok   Bogotá   Caracas   Kuala Lumpur
Lisbon   London   Madrid   Mexico City   Milan   Montreal   New Delhi
Santiago   Seoul   Singapore   Sydney   Taipei   Toronto

The McGraw·Hill Companies

Writing
A PHILOSOPHY STATEMENT
An Educator's Workbook

McGraw-Hill's Custom Publishing consists of products that are produced from camera-ready copy. Peer review, class testing, and accuracy are primarily the responsibility of the author(s).

234567890 QSR QSR 09876

ISBN-13: 978-0-07-293946-0
ISBN-10: 0-07-293946-X

Editor: Judith Wetherington
Production Editor: Carrie Braun
Cover Design: Maggie Lytle
Printer/Binder: Quebecor World

Preface

My approach or philosophical orientation to teaching has been greatly influenced by colleagues from whom I have learned to imagine life's goodness. Among these are my mentor, Nelson L. Haggerson, Jr., emeritus, Arizona State University, and colleague and friend, Joseph P. Braun, Jr. emeritus, Illinois State University. Thank you.

Other colleagues have reminded me to present material in its most complex manner so that students can "study up". I thank Lynn Burlbaw, Frank Clark, and Jack Helfeldt, Texas A&M University, College Station. I also thank Dennie Smith, Department Head, Teaching, Learning and Culture, my talented doctoral student, Rui Kang and the College of Education at A&M. No work would see the light of day without the hard work of an exemplary publisher. I appreciate the work of Judy Wetherington, McGraw-Hill.

This book is dedicated to Brandt W. Pryor. Brandt makes my life happier than I could adequately express. Thanks BW!

To the students I have been honored to teach and those I hope to meet….keep *your heart* in teaching and your philosophy will follow.

Caroline R. Pryor
Texas A&M University
November, 2003

Table of Contents

Section One:
Overview

➢ **Introduction**

➢ **Five Philosophical Approaches**

    Executive Approach

    Humanist Approach

    Subject Specialist Approach

    Citizen Teacher Approach

    Explorer Approach

        ➢ Descriptors of Each Approach
        ➢ Teaching Example

➢ **Test for Understanding**

➢ **Table 1**
    Comparison of Philosophical Approaches

➢ **Table 2**
    Philosophy of Education Scale

Introduction

What is a Philosophy of Education Statement?

A philosophy of education statement is a synthesis of your approach to teaching based on your experiences, values and beliefs about the goal of education and how these goals are best reached. The statement informs the reader of your approach to various aspects of teaching, such as your approach to grading or selection of classroom activities. These approaches have historical derivations and are categorized in this workbook using heuristic (created) terminology. Other approaches and terms can be found in l readings in classical philosophy and philosophy of education. In this workbook, the terms **teaching approach** and **philosophy of education** are used to mean your *philosophical orientation* to educational beliefs, practices and policy.

Your teaching approach or philosophical orientation can be determined by completing several of the activities in this workbook. Once you have completed these activities you will see how a particular philosophical approach guides various strategies that you might use in the classroom. This is the approach you find most practical. However, you will also find that a secondary approach to teaching is also useful to you. This is not uncommon. You might find that you have not highly rated the remaining approaches discussed here. However, these non-highly rated are approaches might be thought of as secondary philosophical orientation that you might employ—however infrequently. Most teachers draw upon philosophical approaches to teaching that describe their world view, that is--their belief in what is important to teach and how to teach it.

In this workbook, you will learn:

- Five approaches to teaching
- Strategies for identifying your approach to teaching
- Strategies for developing your approach into a written philosophy of education statement
- Practical uses for your philosophy statement

This workbook describes five philosophical approaches to teaching. These five approaches have various created titles. The terms used here to describe philosophical approaches to teaching are derived from classic writings in philosophy and education. In the development of these approaches, I draw on the philosophical and curriculum perspectives of Tanner & Tanner, 1995; Oliva, 2000; & Wactler, 1990 in the development and use of the following five terms: **Executive, Humanist, Subject Specialist, Citizen Teacher and Explorer**. Philosophical approaches to teaching or writing a philosophy of education statement have been discussed in other texts such as Feinberg & Soltis (1998) and Fenstermacher & Soltis (1998) and have been instrumental to the development of the terms used here.

Based on these and other readings, philosophical approaches to teaching are interpreted and expanded here and integrate perspectives that consider the role of the teacher in 21st century teaching: globalization of knowledge and responsive citizenship.

These perspectives on philosophical approaches to teaching are presented here, along with classical perspectives, to provide for an added dimension of understandings about the global goal of education and the role of the teacher.

Each of these five philosophical approaches is described in this workbook and includes:

(a) Basic components of each teaching approach, and

(b) Historical and theoretical aspects of each approach.

This workbook provides several activities to support your development of a well-written philosophy of education statement. These activities are:

> **Journals**
> **Interviews**
> **School Case Study Examples**
> **School Practices and Activities**
> **Sample Philosophy of Education Statements**
> **A Philosophy of Education Scale**
> **Tips for Writing and Editing**

Uses of a Philosophy Statement

Understanding your philosophy of education will help you in leadership positions. Learning how others approach teaching can help you mediate grade level and team meeting discussions by providing insights to how group members' beliefs influence their instructional choices. In the case of site-based management, (both in interviewing for a job or in hiring new teachers) a philosophy statement provides information explaining beliefs about school practice. Examples in the philosophy statements provide the reader with a broader understanding of the writer's approach to issues such as classroom management, or grading policies. Almost all school districts require an applicant to write and discuss their approach to teaching. Teachers and administrators need to understand the basic components that comprise each approach.

Your philosophy of education statement can also be used in the application process for graduate school. A philosophy of education statement helps members of a university graduate admission committee understand your response to questions such as: *What is an educated person, What is the role of the teacher*, or *What are the goals of education?* Upon completion of such a program, oral defense or comprehensive exams typically ask candidates to respond to these questions.

As you progress in your career, understanding a colleague's philosophical approach to teaching can be helpful in carrying out various administrative responsibilities. For example in the student teacher-mentor teacher relationship, understanding others' philosophical orientation can generate conversations about expectations of to writing, implementing or evaluating lesson plans. School principals need to understand parental perspectives and educational orientations in order to determine their expectations of school practice. Superintendents need to understand the breadth or comprehensiveness of philosophical approaches across their district.

It is not uncommon for philosophical approaches to change during the life cycle of the teacher-administrator. New experiences or educational exposure can influence decisions about the purpose of education and the role of the teacher. Overall, each individual holds central beliefs about education and these will be evident in your teaching decisions and leadership. Alignment or flexibility with the perspectives of those with whom you work or lead will provide you and your school team with helpful insights and more positive outcomes in working together.

Five Philosophical Approaches

≋ ≋ ≋ ≋ ≋ ≋ ≋ ≋ ≋ ≋ ≋ ≋ ≋ ≋≋ ≋ ≋ ≋ ≋ ≋ ≋ ≋≋ ≋ ≋ ≋ ≋ ≋ ≋ ≋

The EXECUTIVE Approach

This approach is termed *executive* due to an orientation towards traditional efficiency in the classroom. Berliner (1983) found that teachers often approached their teaching as *managers of a business*. Not unlike functionalist concepts underlying a factory model of education (Feinberg & Soltis, 1998), the executive philosophical approach suggests classroom organization with an emphasis on teacher lead instruction, objective types of learning assessment, and rule driven classroom management styles. Instructional design and lesson plans center on quantitative outcomes and the use of questioning strategies such as "What is the right answer"?

In the executive approach to teaching, lesson plans always align with state mandated standards for grade level and are typically organized as direct models of instruction. Teachers who implement an executive philosophy to teaching are skill oriented, efficient in lesson planning, create materials to meet state standards, and teach and test to the objectives of these standards. Nonetheless, the executive approach has been implemented most often historically (e.g. Tyler, 1959) and is often perceived as an efficient approach to teaching (Feinberg & Soltis, 1998). Use of objective tests combined with criterion-referenced grading policies is key to this approach. This approach can be efficient in delivering content to large numbers of students. The goal of education using the executive approach to teaching is *efficient mastery of content*.

Descriptors of an Executive Teacher

➢ Role of the Teacher	Manager
➢ Instructional Approach	Direct instruction
➢ Typical Student Activity	Worksheets
➢ Resources	Based on state standards
➢ View of Knowledge	Basic essential skills
➢ Goal of Education	Mastery of core knowledge

Teaching Example

The executive approach to teaching can be observed in a teacher's classroom management strategies. In this approach the teacher uses their direct authority and control to establish classroom rules and consequences for the infraction of such a rule. One way a teacher accomplishes this task can be seen when students are "off-task" or not following teacher directions. When a teacher begins a lesson and finds students are talking to each other, or are moving around the classroom, this behavior is identified as "off-task" behavior. Given an executive philosophical approach to classroom management, the teacher might immediately respond by moving noisy students to isolated study areas or simply re-arrange classroom desks to eliminate group interaction.

NOTES

The
HUMANIST
Approach

       The *humanist* approach to teaching is centered on the interests and abilities of each student (Tanner & Tanner, 1995). The components of this philosophy include developing pedagogical practice based on various levels of student ability. Historically, educational progressivists (e.g. Rousseau, Froebel, Dewey and others) have sought to include the diverse nature of the developing child into their approach to teaching (Smith, 1984). The objective of the humanist approach is to facilitate the self-actualization of each child (Fenstermacher & Soltis, 1998). However, in order to follow the tenets of humanism, the teacher must be prepared to react to multiple abilities of students and create a classroom environment in which multiple ways of learning are encouraged.

       The humanist teacher approaches teaching by understanding the individual abilities and learning styles of each student. Typically, models of instruction are organized so that each student has an opportunity to select information and equipment that they find interesting to use. The classroom environment is rich with resources that are motivating and exciting to students. These resources expand the content taught in the state standards and build on the interests of each student. Here, the learner chooses the content they want to learn and the manner in which they might indicate they have learned the content. Teachers who use a humanist approach to teaching are student oriented, flexible and innovative in planning lessons and develop a variety of materials to help students meet state standards. They teach in a manner that facilitates each student's understanding of the objectives of state standards. The humanist approach has been used to promote student choice of what to learn and to help students develop an independent approach to learning (e.g., Montessori as cited in Connell, 1980). This approach is often perceived as a supportive and helpful approach to involving student in class work (Feinberg & Soltis, 1998). Portfolios and journals are often used as evidence of learning and self-evaluation rubrics rather than teacher grading are key in this approach. The goal of education using the humanist approach to teaching is *self-actualization as a result of learning.*

Descriptors of a Humanist Teacher.

- ➢ Role of the Teacher   Facilitator

- ➢ Instructional Approach   Student experiences

- ➢ Typical Student Activity   Small interactive groups

- ➢ Resources   Manipulative materials

- ➢ View of Knowledge   Multiple understandings

- ➢ Goal of Education   Self-Actualization

Teaching Example

The humanist approach to teaching can be seen in a teacher's approach to organization of the classroom environment. As a humanist, the teacher uses flexible workstations or centers as small laboratories for student opportunity for exploration and learning. These centers are supplied with materials and resources that can be used in a variety of ways to meet state teaching standards. Here, a student might use a journal to record their observations of a science standard and determine new ways to use materials. Spontaneous conversation with other students at the work center or laboratory is common, but not required. The humanist teacher encourages student decisions about personal learning behavior. Students learn from each other and give support and acknowledgment of various ways of learning. Given a humanist philosophical approach to classroom environment, the teacher might respond to noisy students by finding out what they have discussed at their learning center and ask students to describe this knowledge to the entire class. If a student chooses to work in an isolated study area, this desire is acknowledged and a student is supplied with independent resources.

NOTES

The
SUBJECT
SPECIALIST
Approach

The *subject specialist* approach to teaching is centered on students becoming knowledgeable within a particular domain area (e.g., mathematics, science, or history). The components of this philosophy include developing teaching practices based on the nature of the subject. Here, a teacher's focus is the breadth and depth of the subject area and knowledge of the subject is central to the goal of education. Student interests and various levels of ability are less a consideration in this philosophical approach—rather subject area mastery and thorough understanding is expected. Historically, educational classicists have predetermined which subject areas are most important to teach (e.g., Aristotle, Socrates, and Plato). Subjects such as music, grammar, mathematics, and geography are viewed as "classic" subject areas and are taught to students *in a manner that reflects the main emphasis of the area*. Each area contains fundamental knowledge as well as specific ways of learning this knowledge (Fenstermacher & Soltis, 1998; Hutchins, 1952). The objective of the classicist approach is to ensure a love of learning of the content area, and the predominant mode of instruction is discussion and questioning. Both historical and contemporary knowledge is recognized in this approach, however this knowledge is seen as "core knowledge" and mastery is expected. This approach differs from the executive approach to mastery—the classicist student views learning as pleasure they gain from knowledge of each subject topic.

In the subject-specialist approach, lesson plans are developed from a core of historical-contemporary knowledge. The classicist teacher approaches teaching by understanding the vast amount of subject area information. Typically, instruction is organized so that students use classic books, texts and maps and other resources specific to the subject. These resources highlight the content found in state standards and build on the nature of the subject. In the subject-specialist approach, the learner does not choose the content they want to learn and or the manner in which they might indicate they have learned the content, as the subject construct defines these aspects.

Teachers who implement a subject specialist philosophy to teaching are knowledge oriented, non-flexible and collect vast amounts of information that they can present in their lectures. Rather than devise materials to meet state standards, and teach in a manner that will facilitate each student's understanding of the objectives of state standards. They follow the nature of the subject and expect that students will independently develop habits to enhance subject knowledge. Essays, debate and classroom discussions are often used as evidence of learning. The goal of education in the subject-specialist approach is to *promote a student's love of learning* (Fenstermacher & Soltis, 1998).

Descriptors of a Subject Specialist Teacher

- ➤ Role of the Teacher   Information collector
- ➤ Instructional Approach   Lecture and experiential
- ➤ Typical Student Activity   Discussion and questions
- ➤ Resources   Classic books, texts and maps
- ➤ View of Knowledge   Historical and core knowledge
- ➤ Goal of Education   Love of learning

Teaching Example

The subject-specialist-approach to teaching is evident in practices such as grading policies. In this approach the teacher might incorporate mastery learning into grading. Centers such as small laboratories are used for student exploration. These centers are used for the purpose of *the accumulation of specific knowledge*; Centers are supplied with materials and resources that are specific and particular to a subject. In a reading center, a student might record the number of books they have read. One example of a subject specialist grading policy is to supply students with the Great Books of the Western World (Hutchins, 1952) and check off how many of these particular books a student has read. Students would also be expected to discuss, in depth, the subject of these books. A student's demonstration of their depth and breadth of subject knowledge is evaluated by the teacher and the basis of their grade. Spontaneous conversation with other students at the work center or laboratory is not common—rather conversations are teacher organized and centered on topics found in the Great Books.

Although students might learn from each other, the subject-specialist approach expects the teacher to be a subject area expert. If the teacher is a generalist (as in the case of teaching the Great Books), the teacher is expected to be knowledgeable about all of the information in these books. The grading policy used by the subject-specialist teaching approach provides each student with ample opportunity and time to master the core knowledge of a subject. In practice, this means that a teacher might provide multiple opportunities for a student to write and then re-write an essay, or to read from various sources in order to use reasoned argument in classroom discussion.

NOTES

The CITIZEN TEACHER Approach

The goal of the *citizen teacher* approach is to prepare each student to become an informed participant in a democracy. In this approach, a teacher demonstrates practical examples of the social, historical and economic roles of citizenry. Three principles of democracy define these examples: liberty-freedom, justice-fairness, and equality-equal opportunity (Gutmann, 1987; Pryor, 2002; Pryor & Pryor, 2003). In classroom discussions, students' use of communication (discourse) is encouraged, and the teacher's role is a *prepared participant*. The teacher views this role as would the mayor of a city; listening and prompting discussion and multiple points of view, gathering information to determine decisions, and encouragement of participation of all the city's citizens. The citizen teacher provides for and encourages classroom instruction in which students and teachers debate, and discuss content as well as classroom procedures. One look at this teacher's classroom might make one think of a town hall or committee meeting!

The citizen teacher enjoys providing for class meetings and student (or class) councils. This classroom environment would likely include a wide array of resources that prompt debate, using resources such as newspapers, magazines, and the Internet. This teacher is likely to invite the town mayor or a member of city council to visit the class. In elementary grades, students would be encouraged to ask questions of these guests. The teacher would expect students to be prepared and interested in generating a list of questions to prompt classroom debate—even with a guest present.

The citizen teacher views knowledge as important social and practical resources. For example, the citizen teacher expects that students want to know about how Congress passes a law because these laws will affect their everyday lives. The teacher will expose students to critical, higher order thinking and processes of inquiry. Spelling bees, debate and classroom discussions are often used as evidence of learning. The teacher will use these strategies in all the content areas taught, and students will be expected to voice their opinion, seek out information to support their opinion, and to be active in applying information in their own lives. In short, each member of the class is guided to become *a participant* with personal viewpoints and opinions.

Teachers who implement a citizen teacher philosophy are politically informed, spending vast amounts of time collecting materials from which students can become informed citizens. Rather than devise materials to meet state standards, they teach in a manner that will facilitate each student's exploration and inquiry into the content that meets the objectives of state standards. They expect that parents will perceive this approach to teaching as just and equal for all students, and that the approach provides a foundation for citizenship.

Descriptors of a Citizen Teacher

- ➢ Role of the Teacher   Participant
- ➢ Instructional Approach   Narrative and discursive
- ➢ Student Activity   Class meetings and student council
- ➢ Resources   Newspapers and guest speakers
- ➢ View of Knowledge   Social-practical understandings
- ➢ Goal of Education   Participatory citizen

Teaching Example

Teachers who view their role as a citizen teacher provide their students with numerous leadership roles. Students learn to help others, make decisions, and learn more about self-expression. The citizen teacher uses strategies such as town halls or community circles to solve classroom management problems. They elect a class president and the class council is designed to hear students "tell each side of a problem". This council often functions as a classroom judiciary or mediation panel. Students are not given a set of classroom rules to follow; they develop the rules after much class debate. Teachers function as a guide, helping students discover the practical and useful consequences of their decisions. Citizen teachers do not punish students or threaten then, they involve them!

NOTES

The
EXPLORER
Approach

The *explorer* approach is centered on discovering vast amounts of information; however the use of information in this approach is distinctly different from the term *knowledge* used in the *subject specialist* approach. Unlike the subject specialist, who regards historical and contemporary knowledge for its collective potential, the emphasis of the *explorer* approach to teaching centers is on the rapid change of information. The explorer-teacher seeks to help students understand the changing world and the expanding role of global interaction. An explorer teacher believes the vastness of information precludes any single teacher from "knowing it all".

This definition drastically changes the perspectives a teacher might have on their individual role and the goal of education. The role of the teacher as an explorer is that of an inventor-interpreter of information. In this role, teachers assist students, helping them judge, expand or eliminate information. Teachers and students often work together using technology in a parallel manner, often sharing and correcting the information each has gathered. In so doing, the teacher models how information could be interpreted and discusses the moral dimensions and responsibility of acquired knowledge. The teacher helps students develop the moral filter through which they can evaluate and derive meaning from often-uncensored information.

Teachers who implement an explorer philosophy find resources to help students connect to vast amounts of information. Rather than developing a classroom environment in which students are provided with information (*executive*), guided or mentored (*humanist*), inspired (*subject-specialist*), or debated (*citizen*), here the classroom is organized for exploration. In the process of exploration, students become proficient information finders *and* evaluators of information. They use both a moral filter (good-bad) and a content filter (good-bad) to determine if information is valuable or applicable.

Students in an explorer teacher's classroom share information with classmates *and* with their teachers. Learning typically occurs in a parallel manner, with teachers learning *from* students. Due to the global nature of information, this role reversal is common, with teachers and students interacting and connecting internationally. Students learn to value these connections and become part of a global community of learners. This approach is valued by post-modernist philosophers' perspective that information is ever changing due to re-interpretation of collected findings (Slattery, 1995).

Descriptors of an Explorer Teacher

- ➤ Role of the Teacher   Inventor-interpreter of information
- ➤ Instructional Approach   Exploratory-sense making, web search
- ➤ Typical Student Activity   Web exploration, field trips, personal project
- ➤ Resources for Teacher Use   Technology and multi-media
- ➤ View of Knowledge   Global understanding
- ➤ Goal of Education   Freedom

Teaching Example

The classroom environment of an *explorer* approach to teaching is typically filled with technological equipment, audio-visual aids, and presentation resources. Although the classroom environment appears philosophically *executive* due to the placement of equipment in workstations, the use of equipment is typically collaborative. A teacher might spend an entire class session circulating among students at their stations. Students decide when and how to collaborate with others as they move around the classroom seeking advice, information and showing others how to use equipment. Presentations often highlight newly discovered information or technological tips, as well as content findings. When students seek information from students in other countries, or share information across the web, they process this information through well-defined filters of morality, community, change and information enhancement.

NOTES

☑ *Test for Understanding*

Pre-test
Answer these questions *before* you write your philosophy statement

1. What are the characteristics of an *executive* approach to teaching?
    a. Teacher as classroom manager and planner for students.
    b. Teacher as classroom facilitator and co-planner with students
    c. Teacher as content expert and mentor to students
    d. Teacher as interpreter and consultant to students?

2. What are the characteristics of a *humanist* approach to teaching?
    a. Teacher as classroom manager and planner for students.
    b. Teacher as classroom facilitator and co-planner with students
    c. Teacher as content expert and mentor to students
    d. Teacher as interpreter and consultant to students?

3. What are the characteristics of a *subject specialist* approach to teaching?
    a. Teacher as classroom manager and planner for students.
    b. Teacher as classroom facilitator and co-planner with students
    c. Teacher as content expert and mentor to students
    d. Teacher as interpreter and consultant to students?
    e.
4. What are the characteristics of a *citizen teacher* approach to teaching?
    a. Teacher as classroom manager and planner for students.
    f. Teacher as classroom facilitator and co-planner with students
    g. Teacher as content expert and mentor to students
    h. Teacher as interpreter and consultant to students?

5. What are the characteristics of *explorer* approach to teaching?
    a. Teacher as classroom manager and planner for students.
    b. Teacher as classroom facilitator and co-planner with students
    c. Teacher as content expert and mentor to students
    d. Teacher as interpreter and consultant to students?

NOTES

Post-test
Answer these questions *after* you write your philosophy statement

1. Which of the following descriptors best describes an *executive* approach to classroom environment?
    a. student-oriented
    b. task-oriented
    c. content-oriented
    d. technologically oriented
    e. group process oriented

2. Which of the following descriptors best describes a *humanist* approach to grading/evaluation?
    a. multiple choice tests are used to assess stated objectives
    b. ongoing portfolio assessment
    c. essay exams
    d. quality of use of interactive multi-media (e.g., email)
    e. rubric scoring for debate

3. Which of the following descriptors best describes a *subject specialist* approach to classroom management?
    a. classroom meetings with teacher-student established rules
    b. teacher models desired behavior with each student responsible for conduct
    c. teachers and students use technological interaction to discuss rules
    d. teacher establishes rules with consequences for undesired behaviors
    e. teacher-class meetings to establish rules

4. Which of the following descriptors best describes a *citizen teacher* approach to classroom management?
    a. classroom meetings with teacher-student established rules
    b. teacher models desired behavior with each student responsible for conduct
    c. teachers and students use technological interaction to discuss rules
    d. teacher establishes rules with consequences for undesired behavior
    e. student centered rules with personal consequences

5. Which of the following descriptors best describes an *explorer* approach to classroom activities?
    a. Students work together on-line using multi-media to peer teach and tutor
    b. Students conduct in-depth research after classroom inquiry and lecture
    c. Students work independently using teacher prepared or organized material
    d. Student select their own topics, keeping journals of their activities
    e. Students work together cooperatively toward a group goal

Table 1
Comparison of Philosophical Approaches to Teaching

	Teacher as Executive	Teacher as Humanist	Teacher as Subject Specialist	Teacher as Citizen	Teacher as Explorer
Role of teacher	Manager	Facilitator	Collector	Participant	Inventor-Interpreter
Instructional approach:	Direct Instruction	Student experiences	Lecture and experiential	Narrative and Discursive	Exploratory-sense making, Web search
Activities:	Worksheets	Small interactive groups	Discussion and questions	Class meetings/ student council	Field trips, personal-projects
Resources	Standards-Based	Manipulatives	Classic Books, texts, maps	Newspapers, guest speakers	Technology Multi-media
View of Knowledge	Basic essential skills	Multiple understandings	Historical and core knowledge	Social-practical Understandings	Global understandings
Goal of Education	Mastery of content	Self-actualization	Love of learning	Participatory citizen	Freedom
Exemplar (see appendices for additional examples)	Skinner and Watson Bennett	Montessori Gardner	Hutchins and Adler Conant	Dewey Gutmann	Rousseau Pinar and Slattery

Table 2
Philosophy of Education Scale

Each box below contains describing phrases or words. Score each group of words, giving yourself (5) for the descriptors most like you, (4) the next most like you, (3) the next like you, (2) not like you, and (1) not at all like you. (Score across each category.) Next, rate each individual item in each box using the 5-point scale above. Finally, add scores in each small box in each column (down) to obtain column totals. (Copyright C.R. Pryor, 2003).

CLASSROOM ENVIRONMENT

☐	☐	☐	☐	☐
__ Task-oriented __ Organized/Efficient __ Commercially prepared material	__ Student-oriented __ Flexible activities __ Student-generated material	__ Content-oriented __ Goal-directed/ semi-structured __ Teacher-prepared materials	__ Technology-oriented __ Production-dominated activity __ High use of multi-media	__ Culturally enriched environment with global perspectives __ Safe learning community __ Interactive learning environment

LESSON PLANS

☐	☐	☐	☐	☐
__ Specific objectives and standards clearly defined __ Essential elements of instruction are addressed __ Meets district guidelines, scope and sequence	__ Long-term, broadly structured outcomes __ Thematic and integrated curriculum __ Student-centered learning	__ Emphasis on depth of knowledge __ Instruction extends beyond standardized testing __ Extensive resources (field trips, guest speakers)	__ Open-ended objectives __ Inquiry __ Emphasis on technological skills and information interpreting techniques	__ Flexible goals based on community and citizenship needs __ Practical knowledge and life skills __ Higher-order, critical thinking and problem-solving

CLASSROOM MANAGEMENT

☐	☐	☐	☐	☐
__ Teacher/School-developed rules __ Positive reinforcement for desired behaviors __ Defined consistent consequences for undesired behaviors	__ Classroom meetings and peer review __ Rules established cooperatively by teacher and students __ Serious problems dealt with individually	__ Teacher models desired behaviors __ Self-evaluation on ethics and moral development __ Students responsible for his or her own conduct	__ Individual responsibility is stressed __ Teachers and students discuss expectations __ Procedures govern student interaction with technology	__ Parental involvement in solving problems __ Student input in consequences and guidelines __ Individual rights, community focus, self-responsibility, respect for others

22

Table 2 Continued

ACTIVITIES				
☐ Regular/consistent individual assignments; Lecture-direct instruction; Daily or weekly homework assignments/projects	☐ Journal writing; Cooperative learning; Student-selected activities and projects	☐ In-depth research projects on content areas; Lecture/discussion/inquiry; Extensive reading	☐ Student-teacher share; Peer teaching; Students create presentations and projects	☐ Community service; Leadership development/teamwork skills; Emphasis on diversity in debate/discussion/role play

GRADING/EVALUATION				
☐ Standards-based testing; Objective measurement; Scored evaluation measures	☐ Portfolio assessment; Effort considered as achievement; Self and peers evaluate process as well as products	☐ Essay and objective tests; Ability to apply knowledge as achievement; Thorough and rigorous standards	☐ Graded on level of decision-making, resources used and application; Evidence of technological competence; Feedback and evaluation often given in electronic formats	☐ Evaluation based based on contribution to civic responsibilities; Student/teacher jointly developed rubrics; Immediate feedback, justification/interpretation of grades

KNOWLEDGE/INSTRUCTION				
☐ Step-by-Step instruction; Individual practice; Focus on mastering basic skills and standards	☐ Discovery and personal experiences; Manipulation experimentation/inquiry; Students construct personal understanding of content	☐ Intense study of content area; Perspectives of knowledge important; Breadth of knowledge important	☐ Students search for information; Exploration of knowledge; Interpretation of meaning	☐ Student discovery, inquiry/critique, research projects; Understanding of democratic process; Practical knowledge equals content knowledge

TEACHER'S ROLE				
☐ Manager; Organizer; Planner	☐ Facilitator; Inquirer; Co-Learner	☐ Expert; Mentor; Guide	☐ Interpreter; Consultant; Connector	☐ Leader; Citizen; Patriot

Column total	Column Total	Column Total	Column Total	Column Total

Section Two:
Identifying Your Philosophical Approach

➢ **Collecting Personal Artifacts**
➢

  Creating a Professional Journal
   Creating a Biographical Journal
   Interviewing
   Administrator-Principal
   Mentor Teacher
   Professor
   Other Teachers

➢ **Case Study Examples**

➢ **Philosophical Approaches in School Practices and Activities**

➢ **Sample Philosophy of Education Statements**

Collecting Personal Artifacts

📖 Tips for Developing a Professional Journal

Use the space below to create lists of educational practices and activities that you like most and least

Example

Identify the practices-activities that you liked most and least <u>when you were a K-12 student</u>

      Like most   Independent free reading time
      Like least   Pop quiz or test

Example

Identify those practices- activities that you like most and least now, <u>as an educator</u>

      Like most   Hands on activities for discovery
      Like least   Worksheets

Practices and Activities I Like Most
As an educator

As a student

Practiced and Activities I Like Least
As an educator

As a student

📖 Tips for Writing a Professional Journal

> ➤ Explain the practices-activities listed in your like most and least *as an educator* section.
> ➤ Describe how the most-least activities affect teaching and learning.
> ➤ Identify the philosophical approaches of each activity.

Example Journal Entry

I used role-play as an activity to encourage student understanding of the tensions and political concerns during the period before the Revolutionary War. I read to my students and included perspectives of John and Abigail Adams and Thomas Jefferson. Then, I modeled a role-play activity. By reading letters from Abigail to John, I pretended to be Abigail. The students really liked this activity and so did I!

I think the reason they liked it is that the perspectives of the historical figurers became real to them; they saw how important Abigail was to John and how he listened to her views. I then asked one student to pretend to be Thomas Jefferson and I took the role of John Adams. We used interview questions. My students liked trying out role-play strategies before they had to research and create their roles. The philosophical orientation of this approach is subject specialist, but it is also humanist. It takes on two philosophical approaches.

📖 Tips for Writing a Biographical Journal

> ➤ Explain each of the practices-activities listed in your likes most and least *as a K-12 student* section.
> ➤ Describe how the most-least activities affect teaching and learning.
> ➤ Identify the philosophical approaches of each activity.

Example Journal Entry

We had been using maps and globes to learn about geographical regions. One of the activities our teacher organized for us was a cooperative learning activity; we were to create our own United States map with a flour-water compound. After we configured the map, we were going to paint it to identify each of the states, rivers, mountains and other identifying aspects of a region. Unfortunately, my group was smaller than the others (only 3 people) so we really had to work hard to finish it up. I remember being excited about using the maps to find places and wanted my group to hurry up and finish the flour-water part so we could find things like the rivers and mountains.

The two other students were having fun making the map out of flour. I was not having fun doing this, and had hoped they would finish up so our map could dry. I didn't really even want to paint the map. I wanted to find things on the real map and put in the small pins to show all the points on the map. I had hoped to find more states, rivers, mountains than any other group, and my group members really just liked the hands-on part. When I became a teacher, I didn't use a lot of hands-on activities unless I thought my students would learn a great deal of new information from the activity. This is a subject-specialist philosophy and I like it best.

Tips for Interviewing

➢ Identify someone at your school or district that might describe approach to teaching. If you are an intern or student teacher, you might want to interview your mentor teacher or the school principal. If you are a principal, you might want to interview three other principals. You might interview your professor, or other teachers. Ask your principal before you interview parents.

➢ Explain the purpose and amount of time needed.

➢ Prepare a list of questions before the interview.
The most-least liked activities are an effective sample interview questions.

➢ Take notes during the interview and use clarifying questions.

➢ Ask the interviewee to describe what they think is effective approaches to teaching.

➢ Ask what they would change about teaching and learning with classes in the future.

➢ Summarize the interview findings. Write those finding below.

Interview Results

Interview #1

Title of Person Interviewed	Responsibility	Grade Level

Main points learned in the interview

Philosophy of Education of the person interviewed

Your reflections on philosophy of the person interviewed

Interview #2
Title of Person Interviewed   **Responsibility**   **Grade Level**

Main points learned in the interview

Philosophy of Education of the person interviewed

Your reflections on philosophy of the person interviewed

CASE STUDY
Five Approaches to Grading

Beliefs or philosophical approaches to teaching can be seen in policies, practices and activities used in schools. As you work with other teachers, administrators and parents, their philosophical approaches will become evident to you. As you reflect on your own philosophy of education, you will respond to choices about school practice and the desires of others to employ a similar-different practice. Case studies are one way to practice evaluating your philosophy of education in the context of a school practice.

Read the case studies below and determine (a) which of the five philosophic approaches best represents each teacher or principal, and (b) how you might respond to each individual based on each of the five philosophical approaches portrayed in this book.

How Should We Evaluate Students at River Middle School?

River Middle School is meeting to discuss grading policies among the faculty in a multi-content department. These department teams are composed of mathematics, language arts (reading), science, social studies and computer science teachers. This faculty is responding to concerns from parents that the school should meet the diverse and multilingual needs of the community and consider the growth and development of students in grading. However, standardized test scores of students at River Middle School are average, and there is concern about the below average scores. The faculty believes it is making good progress towards developing an exceptional teaching team. They are concerned that their grading policies might not represent *the progress* made by all students. Each faculty member views his or her approach to meeting this need differently.

Ms. Smith

Mrs. Smith has been teaching middle school mathematics for seven years. Her approach to teaching reflects a perspective that all students learn best if they are involved in their own learning. She implements this belief by providing students with mathematics manipulatives and cooperative learning opportunities. She expects students to share their knowledge, decide on their own learning objectives, and select a strategy to portray their own learning. Rather than use worksheets for homework, students keep a journal that indicates strengths and weaknesses in mathematics. She grades each student on the progress they have made toward their learning objective. In order to report formal progress on a report card, Ms. Smith uses a letter grade, and includes a letter to parents describing the students' progress

Mrs. Smith's philosophic approach is_____

Select words or phrases used in this teacher's approach that explain this philosophy
List these here: _____   _____

_____   _____

Mr. Linequest

Mr. Linequest has been teaching middle school science for 18 years. He believes that all students learn best if they are provided with direct instruction with clear learning objectives. Many of his students take high school level science while they are still in middle school, and eventually advanced high school placement courses. Mr. Linequest has taken additional science courses and developed a curriculum directly linked to advancing students' expertise. His goal is to provide an efficient process for teaching science.

He implements his beliefs by providing students with in-depth practice using materials such as worksheets, quizzes and tests, and direct questioning during classroom explanations. Mr. Linequest believes these activities gives students immediate feedback about their skills and helps them stay on task. Mr. Linequest grades each student on several variables: work turned in on time, neatness of work, and correctness of answers. To calculate students' grades, he uses a 10-point grading scale. Scores of assigned work are calculated and students receive the grade they have earned. Mr. Linequest believes this method is fair to all students.

Mr. Linequest's philosophic approach is_____

Select words or phrases used in this teacher's approach that support this philosophy
List these here: _____   _____

_____   _____

Mrs. Chavier

Mrs. Chavier has been teaching at the middle school level for three years, and is a former school librarian. She believes that all students learn best if they are provided rich resources for learning. Her classroom contains 2,000 books. She has collected these books from libraries, book fairs and garage sales. Mrs. Chavier hopes that her students love reading as much as she does. Her students participate in activities such as making their own book, peer reading and reporting about books, and reading aloud to parents. Many of Mrs. Chavier's students are reading to parents who are non-readers of English. These parents are active in the reading program and Mrs. Chavier provides all students with a lending library of books to take home. Although her students score well on standardized tests, Mrs. Chavier does not grade students only using standard measures. She expects students to document their reading progress and she has developed a rubric for this documentation. Mrs. Chavier allows for mastery learning before grading—working on a skill until mastery is achieved. Students record their progress in reading on their reading progress chart. Mrs. Chavier uses a 10-point grading scale. After she calculates the reading grade, and she adds 10 percent to the score for student effort. She believes this method indicates both skill and desire to become a good reader.

Mrs. Chavier's philosophic approach is_____

Select words or phrases used in this teacher's approach that support this philosophy
List these here: _____   _____

_____   _____

Mr. West

Mr. West is a first year teacher who was a software developer before he became a teacher. He believes that for students to become good consumers of information, they need to learn to gather and evaluate vast amounts of materials. His classroom is arranged in small work centers, all of which include computers and innovative hardware. He has written two technology grants to supply his classroom with equipment. His approach to teaching includes: small group exploration, individual inquiry and evaluation of information, and large group discussion regarding the importance and use of information. Mr. West helps students develop a personal framework for evaluating information (e.g., learning citation rules and how to verify information). Mr. West uses two types of formats for grading: quality of information gathered (rubric developed for grading) and innovation in technological investigation (rubric developed for grading). Mr. West adds five percent to this base grade for student application of practical or conceptual knowledge. Mr. West believes he is preparing students to become independent thinkers with a broad understanding of their own mode of learning and style of exploration.

Mr. West's philosophic approach is_____

Select words or phrases used in this teacher's approach that support this philosophy
List these here: _____   _____

_____   _____

Mrs. Easterly

Mrs. Easterly has been teaching social studies for six years at the middle school and is an active member of her community. She believes that the goal of education is to prepare students to participate in a democratic society. Her class participates in many service-learning projects that involve volunteer work within the community. Students in her class are taught to seek out information about social issues and develop skill in discussion and debate. Mrs. Easterly and her class use multiple resources such as newspapers, guest speakers, and information from web searches to prompt their learning about social-practical issues. Students in this class are expected to use written and oral narrative to explain historical events; essays and class debates are common activities.

Mrs. Easterly uses two types of formats for grading: *appropriateness* of information gathered (which is graded using a rubric) and evidence of inference on how the information informs social policy (graded using a rubric). Historical fact knowledge alone will not be enough to receive a high grade; students need to provide evidence that the information gathered has beneficial social implications. Mrs. Easterly adds 15 % to the rubric grade for student application of knowledge to a service-learning project that benefits the community. Mrs. Easterly believes she is preparing students to become knowledgeable and prepared citizens of a democracy.

Mrs. Easterly's philosophic approach is_____

Select words or phrases used in this teacher's approach that support this philosophy
List these here: _____   _____

_____   _____

Philosophical Approaches in School Practices and Activities

Lesson Plan Components

      The checklists below can help you identify the philosophical approach of particular practices and activities. These practices and activities are commonly found in the instructional section of lesson plans. Sometimes the practices might be found in the lesson objective, or closure section of the lesson. Lesson plans can be evaluated by the philosophical components used within each plan.

      For example, are group work activities an executive or humanist instructional step? Is grading using objective tests an executive or explorer approach?

☑ **Complete each checklist and then use the note section for your explanations.**

Executive Approach

Identify executive practices used as "set" or "motivation" in a lesson plan.

Place an "x" next to each executive practice.

    __ Teacher uses a pop-quiz to determine student knowledge
    __ Students read aloud from their journal
    __ Students try out a new laboratory procedure for later use
    __ Students describe a recent field trip.
    __ Instantaneous outcomes and communication from a technologically organized project is explored
    __ Answers to homework are projected so students can get information quickly
    __ A guest speaker describes the benefits of service learning
    __ Teacher lists frequently missed questions the previous homework
    __ Students have books open and await further instruction
    __ Teacher reads a newspaper story to motivate class discussion
    __ Students discuss possible uses various resources in classroom
    __ Computers are used for pre test for the upcoming chapter material
    __ Student opinions are elicited for exploration of interesting topics

NOTES

Humanist Approach

Identify humanist classroom practices.

Place an "x" next to each humanist practice.

__ Teacher assigns students to a group and hands out worksheets
__ Study guides and the teacher prepares outlines
__ Students select a laboratory partner and work on project together
__ Students keep a journal of group laboratory work and make group decisions
__ Instantaneous outcomes and communication are technologically organized
__ Email is used for questions and dialogue
__ Student study groups are used for questions and dialogue
__ Self and peer evaluation is common
__ Students are required to take detailed notes of lecture
__ Teacher uses "lock-step" direct instructional procedures
__ Students determine how to use various resources in classroom
__ Computers are used for group or individual exploration of interesting topics

NOTES

Subject Specialist Approach

Identify the instructional objectives of a subject specialist lesson plan.

Place an "x" next to each subject-speciailist objective.

__ The student will identify five plant species

__ The student will explain the difference between growth and development using examples and counter-examples.

__ The student will locate five plant species web sites and route these to group members

__ The student will write an essay describing the history of agriculture in the United States and its impact on technological development.

__ The student will complete a multiple choice pre-test with 100% accuracy

__ The student will meet with group members to determine individual tasks for a group project

__ The student will correctly list and define 100% of the vocabulary words in chapter three

__ The student will keep a journal of the activities used in laboratory work

__ The student will read six books that compare and contrast the causes of the civil war and be able to represent historical argument in class

__ The student will peer coach and edit three group members' selection of web sites.

NOTES

Citizen Teacher Approach

Identify the instructional objectives of a citizen teacher lesson plan.

Place an "x" next to each citizen teacher objective.

__ The student will be able to identify five examples of mammals

__ The student will be able to explain the economic development of state
   regions using examples and counterexamples.

__ The student will be able to locate five plant species web sites and route these to
   group members

__ The student will be able to write an essay describing the history of agriculture
   in the United States and its impact on technological development.

__ The student will be able to complete a multiple choice pre-test with 100% accuracy

__ The student will complete individual tasks for a group project

__ The student will correctly list and define 100% of the vocabulary words in
   chapter three

__ The student will contribute to their community in a service learning activity

__ The student will read six books that compare and contrast the causes of the civil war
   and be able to represent historical argument in class

__ The student will peer coach and edit three group members' selection of web sites.

NOTES

Explorer Approach

Identify the instructional steps of an explorer lesson plan.

Place an "x" next to each explorer instructional step

___ Tell students to copy 50 vocabulary works from a list found in a book chapter
___ Ask students to use hands-on materials and keep a journal of student contributions to groups findings
___ Lecture for 45 minutes on the dates and outcomes of World War II battles
___ Ask students to form debate teams, and grade students on discourse skills
___ Administer a mandatory mid-term multiple-choice exam using the information from the teacher's lecture notes.
___ Provide students with email access to find a "study buddy" in another country
___ Provide students with worksheets to complete in a 45 minute class session.
___ During lecture, suggest ways that students might engage in debate.
___ Ask students to demonstrate to the class how they have integrated the use of technology into their research process.
___ Ask a student to show you how they integrated audio into a power point presentation.
___ Administer a timed "pop" quiz on information taught the previous day
___ List ten topics in history that interest students. Ask students to divide into project teams and respond to eight pre-determined questions.

NOTES

Sample Philosophy of Education Statements

A philosophy of educations statement can range in length from one paragraph to two to three pages. Below are samples of short, one-paragraph statements that are typically used on a job application. This length may vary however, and longer statements might be required by a school district or in graduate school applications. These short examples are designed to help you recognize philosophical approaches to teaching.

If you are a district administrator or campus principal, you will want to identify key words in the statement in order to understand to approach used by an applicant. If you are applying for a job, or to graduate school, or completing comprehensive exams after completing graduate courses, understanding how to make sense of a written philosophical statement will give you insight to the writer's beliefs about best practice. The section in this book--"How to Write a Philosophy of Education Statement" will help you develop your statement.

Executive Sample

I believe the role of the teacher is to prepare students with skills and abilities to compete in society. School is like a full time job for students. Here they learn the habits of completing a job correctly and on time. Teachers are responsible for helping students develop these habits. Students learn best when they have information that is clear and focused and feedback that tells them how well or poorly they have achieved. I use grades to let students know where they stand and what they need to work at to improve. I also provide weekly tests and scores so that they can adjust their study skills benefit from direct feedback. In my classroom, I stick to a schedule and keep the class running smoothly

The goal of education is to provide graduates who are well prepared to contribute to society. These skills and abilities are contributions that enhance society's economic and social goals. Wealth, health, and conditions of living are all improved by the skills of an educated population.

Humanist Sample

I believe the role of the teacher is to prepare each individual to self-actualize—to become a well-rounded and caring person. I believe school is a place where a teacher can model dignity and self-esteem and where students learn to care about each other. When students work together, they learn about how to share, support and receive information from one another. School is not only about learning information; it is about how to live. I use peer-grading and self-report methods of grading and focus much of my time on helping each student achieve objectives that show their best work. In this manner, I indicate to them that they are an important contributor to society.

The goal of education is to teach interaction and trust within society, I guide my students on an individual basis and provide them with multiple ways of learning. I use multi-cultural perspectives, materials, and parental involvement as enriching activities. Schools should teach children to mentor and facilitate the possibilities within all people. Well-rounded students contribute to a global society and enhance our world.

Subject Specialist Sample

The role of the teacher is to motivate students to become understand that knowledge is the backbone of society. The depth and breadth of a particular knowledge area (such as science or history) provides a world of information that is never ending. A true scholar never stops seeking more information and consumes this information in a manner befitting their area. Science students are inquirers and history students tend to compare and contrast information. Teachers should provide students with a wealth of information so they can learn all they can about the wonderful content areas they are studying. This is a lifelong process—which I have always enjoyed. I show my love of learning to students through the many materials I have collected and by letting them know that I continue to enroll in classes to learn more. I hope they become life-long learners.

The goal of education is to educate students who are knowledgeable about many content areas. Students should learn deeply in several areas (such as mathematics and science) but should not be limited to these areas. A broad, comprehensive education is a *must* for every educated person. By learning from classic works (such as the "Great Books") and from currently developed information, students contribute to the world by becoming informed and responsive to poor information. Teachers and schools have an obligation to educate students in all areas of the curriculum.

Citizen Teacher Sample

The role of the teacher is to help students develop the knowledge and dispositions of a citizen prepared to participate to a democratic society. It is important to me that my students learn to become fair and just in making decisions. To do this they must understand the value of liberty and freedom, and be prepared to see these values upheld in an equal manner for all. Several of the activities that I use help to promote these beliefs: essay writing, classroom discussions and debate, and comparison and contrast of ideas. My role as a teacher is to help students develop their skills of participation—in applying knowledge they have learned and applying knowledge for the good of society.

The goal of education is to ensure the continuation of a democratic society. To address the needs of this society, citizens must be prepared to contribute and understand the assumptions behind each of their decisions. Education is not just about learning the laws or how to vote, it is about understanding the outcomes of decisions behind a vote. This is an educated citizen!

Explorer Sample

The role of the teacher is to model strategies of personal exploration and discovery. I see myself as an inventor who teaches students about various media and technologies to invent the future. Students are free to explore in my classroom. I am interested in their discoveries, and how they use media to learn. I encourage multiple ways of learning—such as field trips to find out information, or personal or group projects in which students connect various types of information.

The goal of education is to ensure that exploration never stops. I believe that there is more information out there than I can teach—and students should be encouraged to become the discoverers of information. The goal of education is to continue exploration so that the lives of all might be enhanced by discovery.

Notes and Explanations

Section Three:
Organizing Your Data

➤ **Personal Artifacts**

➤ **Journal Data**

➤ **Interview Data**

➤ **Case Study Example**

➤ **Results of the Philosophy of Education Scale**

Organizing Your Data

Personal Artifacts

Journal Data

In your two journals—professional and biographical—you have written about various aspects of school and schooling that indicate your philosophical preferences. The word-phrases you used in your journal can tell you about your or approach to teaching.

Use these two steps to understand the information in your journal.

- ➤ Highlight words-phrases that indicate a philosophical approach
- ➤ Write these selected word-phrases on the next page
- ➤ Next to each word-phrase, write the letter symbol for each philosophical approach

Executive	**E**
Humanist	**H**
Subject Specialist	**S**
Citizen teacher	**CL**
Explorer	**EXP.**

Find out more about your philosophical approach!

Symbol Process

Count   the number of symbols.

Are you an Executive? A Humanist? A Subject Specialist?

Grouping Process

List   the Philosophy Scale categories:

Classroom Environment	**Lesson Plans**	**Classroom Environment**	
Activities	**Grading/Evaluation**	**Knowledge/Instruction**	**Teacher's Role**

In which category are you an Executive? A Citizen Teacher? An Explorer?

Write Your Word-phrases and Categories Here.

Professional Journal Data

Biographical Journal Data

Interview Data

You have interviewed several people that are important to you in your developing career. You might have several pages of data about a fellow teacher or a mentor teacher and short notes only from a campus principal or fellow administrator.

To find out more about each person's philosophy, use the <u>symbol or grouping process</u> (see above section) to organize your interview data

Follow these steps:
- ➢ List important words and phrases.
- ➢ Place a **symbol (E, H, S, C, EXP)** next to each highlighted word-phrase.
- ➢ **Categorize** selected word-phrases by symbol (all the E's together) or by category (all word-phrases about grading together)

Interview #1

Name   **Position**   **Years in Profession**

Philosophical Approach _____

Interview #2

Name   **Position**   **Years in Profession**

Philosophical Approach _____

Interview #3

Name   **Position**   **Years in Profession**

Philosophical Approach _____

Interview #4

Name   **Position**   **Years in Profession**

Philosophical Approach _____

Case Study Example

You have gathered data in journals about your own biographical and professional approaches to teaching. You have also gathered data about other individual's philosophical approaches. Which word-phrases are important to you?

Create your own short case study about approaches to teaching. You might want to write about the school's grading policy or testing concerns. Do you want to write about parental involvement and expectations of teachers?

Follow these steps in writing your case study:

> ➢ Write two to three paragraphs that tell about the school setting
> ➢ Describe the various philosophical approaches to the case
> ➢ Resolve the case using your philosophical approach
> ➢ Develop some ways to resolve the case by integrating the philosophical approaches of other people involved in the school

Write your case here:

Case Study

Results of the Philosophy of Education Scale

Data from your use of the Philosophy of Education Scale (POES) can be another indicator of your approach to teaching. To determine your philosophical score, add the total score in the small boxes inside each box by column (down). The columns represent each of the five approaches. You might find that the scores on the scale appear close together—with little difference in overall score. It is not impossible for someone to score 18 as an Executive and 21 as an Explorer. These close scores likely indicate that you have an overriding philosophic approach as an Explorer, with high interest in the Executive approach. The other three approaches might be of use to you only in particular circumstances, such as working with your grade level team, or with parents.

The scores on your POES are another indicator of your philosophy of education. Along with the data gathered in your journals and in interviews, the POES will give you more information about approaches that are important to you.

How to Interpret Your Scores:

Use the Philosophy of Education Scale in this Workbook

Total your scores (down the column) to determine your first and second most highly rated philosophical approach

Find the categories that contain your first and second highly rated approaches. Are you an E in classroom management, but EXP in classroom activities?

List the activities in each category that you have highly rated. Did you highly rate tests and worksheets? Group activities?

Step 1
For each category, list the approach that you have ranked highly (5) or slightly highly (4).

Example: In the Classroom Environment Category
I scored   5 in the Executive approach
                4 in the Humanist approach

Step 2
Look again at these two highly rated approaches.
Which activities or practices did you rate highly (5) or slightly highly (4)?

Example: In the Classroom Environment Category..........
I rated these activities most highly:

Executive	Humanist
5 task-oriented as 5	3 student oriented
4 organized/efficient as	4 flexible activities

Category: *Classroom Environment* (partial example only)

__Task-oriented __Organized/Efficient __Commercially Prepared material	☐	__Student-oriented __Flexible activities __Student-generated Material	☐	__Content-oriented __Goal-directed/ Semi-structured __Teacher-prepared Material	☐

You can see that you have highly rated the executive approach, and you also highly rated task-oriented and organized/efficient activities. You can also see your second most highly rated approach and the activities rated second most highly.

You now have information about your approach as an executive or humanist <u>for the category of classroom environment</u>. However, you might find you use different approaches in the grading category.

Did you expect that you would score highly in a particular approach(es) or with the use of particular activities in a category? For example, did you think you were an "executive" in classroom management" and a humanist in grading?
.
You will now be able to determine which of the approaches contain practices and activities that match with your philosophic approach.

Enter Your Results Here

My Executive Categories and Practices-Activities

Category_____   **Rating** ___

Practices-Activities rated very highly or highly

_____   _____   _____   _____

Category_____   **Rating** ___

Practices-Activities rated very highly or highly

_____   _____   _____   _____

Reflection: Are these activities and practices in which you expected to score highly? Why or why not?

My Humanist Categories and Practices-Activities

Category_____   Rating ___

Practices-Activities rated very highly or highly

_____   _____   _____   _____

Category_____   Rating ___

Practices-Activities rated very highly or highly

_____   _____   _____   _____

Reflection: Are these activities and practices in which you expected to score highly?
Why or why not?

My Subject Specialist Categories and Practices-Activities

Category_____   Rating ___

Practices-Activities rated very highly or highly

_____   _____   _____   _____

Category_____   Rating ___

Practices-Activities rated very highly or highly

_____   _____   _____   _____

Reflection: Are these activities and practices in which you expected to score highly?
Why or why not?

```
┌─────────────────────────────────────────────────────────────────┐
│                                                                   │
│         My Citizen Teacher Categories and Practices-Activities    │
│                                                                   │
│   Category_____          Rating ___           │
│                                                                   │
│   Practices-Activities rated very highly or highly                │
│                                                                   │
│   _____    _____    _____    _____                │
│                                                                   │
│   Category_____          Rating ___           │
│                                                                   │
│   Practices-Activities rated very highly or highly                │
│                                                                   │
│   _____    _____    _____    _____                │
│                                                                   │
│                                                                   │
└─────────────────────────────────────────────────────────────────┘
```

Reflection: Are these activities and practices in which you expected to score highly? Why or why not?

```
┌─────────────────────────────────────────────────────────────────┐
│                                                                   │
│         My Explorer Categories and Practices-Activities           │
│                                                                   │
│   Category_____          Rating ___           │
│                                                                   │
│   Practices-Activities rated very highly or highly                │
│                                                                   │
│   _____    _____    _____    _____                │
│                                                                   │
│   Category_____          Rating ___           │
│                                                                   │
│   Practices-Activities rated very highly or highly                │
│                                                                   │
│   _____    _____    _____    _____                │
│                                                                   │
│                                                                   │
└─────────────────────────────────────────────────────────────────┘
```

Reflection: Are these activities and practices in which you expected to score highly? Why or why not?

Section Four:

How to Write a Philosophy of Education Statement

> ➤ **Tips to the Writing Process**
>   Six *Fast* paragraph starters
>   Four *Quick* editing tips

> ➤ **Peer Editing**
>   Peer writing and coaching
>   Revisions of your statement

How To Write A Philosophy of Education Statement

Six *Fast* Paragraph Starters

Use the following six components in your philosophy statement:

- ➤ **Paragraph One**
  Describe the community you lived in as your school experiences in grades K-12.

- ➤ **Paragraph Two**
  Explain the goal of education

- ➤ **Paragraph Three**
  Describe the role of the teacher

- ➤ **Paragraph Four**
  Describe sample activities that indicate your philosophical approach to teaching

- ➤ **Paragraph Five**
  Describe your approach to classroom environment, management and grading-evaluation

- ➤ **Paragraph Six**
  Explain your personal and professional goals as a teacher

Paragraph One: Community and Schooling

Paragraph Two: Goal of Education

Paragraph Three: Role of the Teacher

Paragraph Four: Sample Activities

Paragraph Five: Classroom Environment, Management and Grading-Evaluation

Paragraph Six: Personal-Professional Goals

Edit and Review your Philosophy of Education Statement

Four *Quick* Tips to Editing

Tip #1   **Parallel Writing**
        In this workbook, you have developed numerous ways to determine your philosophical approach to teaching. You should be familiar now with how each of these approaches represents your beliefs about teaching. Review each of the above six paragraphs. Check each paragraph for words and phrases indicating your first and second most important approaches. These approaches might have changed from your early biographical or professional experiences. You might indicate this change in the statement. It is important that your writing represents past, present and future tenses. In paragraphs two through six you should explain your philosophy of education and it's implications for practice.

Examples:
Paragraph One:
"I grew up thinking that schooling was only about achievement, but I now believe..."

Paragraph Two:
"I believe that the goal of education is to....."

Tip #2   **Add a *new* paragraph or add to paragraph length**
        You might want to add a second paragraph to a section of your philosophy statement. For example, you might want to add detail to some of the practices and activities that are important to you—*add a new* paragraph, *after* paragraph four. If you do this, be certain to: (a) connect the two paragraphs, and (b) use new or different information in the new paragraph

Example:
Paragraph Four:
"These activities are indicators of my executive approach".

Added Paragraph to this section.
"There are several activities that I use to involve students in their own learning. These are humanist focused because they allow students to select research topics of their own choice. My goal is for students to discover a topic that they find interesting.

Expanded Paragraph Four:
" I use several other types of humanist activities such as cooperative learning, self-selected reports, and peer-editing".

Note: If you use the descriptor words (executive, humanist and others) be certain to use a short explanation of each term.

Tip #3   Use an Active Voice

Most writing manuals suggest using an active writing voice. An active writing voice portrays importance and conviction of belief, an important aspect in a clear philosophy of education statement. Use the present not the past tense (except for the biographical paragraph)

Examples:

> Write *"I believe..."* instead of *...*"the beliefs I have are"

> Write *"I consider"* instead of ...*"I have considered"*

> Use a confident style. Write, *"My goals are..."*

> Do not use an aggressive style....
  Do not write, *"This is what is wrong with education"*

> Use *active* words. Write... *"I implement ..."*

> Avoid qualifying words...
  Do not write "I consider parents *very* important,
  Write, **"Parents are important"**.

Active words focus attention on the writer rather than on the reader, and convey direct and clear communication.

Example Active Words:

arrange	discover	improvise	program
accomplish	document	implement	prepare
activate	encourage	improve	promote
advise	engage	install	plan
collaborate	engage	measure	simplify
coordinate	help	organize	support

Resources for Writing

- ➢ Johnson, A. P. (2002). *A Short Guide to Action Research*. Boston: Allyn & Bacon.

- ➢ *Publication Manual of the American Psychological Association* (5th ed.). (2001). Washington, DC: American Psychological Association.

- ➢ Wactler, C.R. (1990). How student teachers make sense of student teaching: The derivations of an individual's educational philosophy. (Doctoral dissertation, Arizona State University, 1990). *Dissertation Abstracts International 51*, 2627.

- ➢ Wolcott, H. F. (2001). *Writing Up Qualitative Research*. Thousand Oaks, CA: Sage.

Tip #4 Peer Editing
Peer editing is a strategy for reviewing a colleague's writing so that you each receive detailed and specific feedback for improvement.

Use the Following Steps to Peer-edit Your Philosophy of Education Statement

- ➢ Read the philosophy of education statement thoroughly

- ➢ Place philosophical approach (E, H, S. CL, & EXP) marks next to the key words and phrases used by the writer.

- ➢ Review these approach marks with the writer. Does the writer agree with your markings?

- ➢ Decide on changes to clarify writing

- ➢ Ask the writer to re-draft any unclear sections, and re-read the draft.

Revision of your Philosophy of Education Statement
Reading a colleague's philosophy of education statement is an effective way to learn about the revision process. It gives you the opportunity to read words used by others to express beliefs that might be helpful in your own re-writing process. Ask your colleague to use the above steps to edit your philosophy statement and then revise your statement. If your markings are not the same as those of the writer, decide on changes to make the writing clear

Use this section for notes for revising your philosophy statement

Section Five:
Practical Uses of a Philosophy of Education Statement

➢ *School Leadership and Administration*
  Your organization's mission statement
  Leading with a philosophy statement

➢ *Job Interviews*
  How to conduct an interview
      The Administrator
      The Job Applicant
      Sample questions and responses
      Peer practice sessions

➢ *Graduate School Applications*
  What are the main points to include?
  Interviewing using your philosophy statement

➢ *Staff Development*
  Identify participants' philosophical approach
  Develop group goals that everyone likes!
  Invent a common vision

School Leadership and Administration

Your Organization's Mission statement

A mission statement is often mistaken for a philosophy statement. They are different! The purpose of a mission statement is to portray a vision that will encompass the multiple perspectives of a particular constituency. A philosophy of education statement is written to explain an individual's personal perspectives on teaching and learning from the author's point of view.

School district mission statements usually describe the breadth of the district goals: "As a K-12 unified district, we believe ..." and the broad purposes of educational work, "We provide a broad, comprehensive, and equal educational opportunity to all students..." The mission statement insures that all members of the district's constituency are represented in the statement ("with support from our business and parental community"). These statements are meant to capture the direction and spirit of a district, rather than the specific strategies that will be implemented ("as a 50 year old district, we hope to continue a tradition of an excellent education for all students...").

The mission statement should give important information about the strength and values held by the district. Most mission statements are written by groups representing the entire school district community and adopted by representative vote. After reviewing a district's mission statement, an individual can write his or her own perspectives of the values portrayed in the statement of mission. This personal perspective becomes the writer's philosophy statement. A short mission statement might be selected by a district and used as a district-wide theme or a mission statement might be more explanatory—and describe global outcomes. The decision to create a short or long mission statement is a matter of style.

Mission Statement Examples:

The goal of Shadow River School District is to provide a comprehensive education for all students in grades K-12.

All students in the Shadow River School District will be provided with a comprehensive education that will prepare them as lifelong learners who contribute to and benefit from their community, nation, and the world.

Activity

List words and phrases in your district's mission statement that represent your philosophy of education. Eliminate those that do not represent your philosophical approach. What words or phrases would you change?

District Mission Statement

Words-Phrases Like My Philosophy   **Words-Phrases Not Like My Philosophy**

Using a Philosophy Statement in Educational Leadership

Educational leaders --elementary principal or district assistant superintendent of curriculum and other positions within a school-department head of biology at a high school, or fourth grade level team leader must understand the various perspectives held by the members with whom they will work. In the case of district wide leadership, the philosophical perspectives of other leaders will bring multiple perspectives to bear on a district concern or initiative. At the school campus level, these same understandings might influence the implementation of a policy or program.

All educational leaders should begin any group change process by understanding the philosophical approach to teaching and learning of each members of the group.

There are several quick ways to learn about these perspectives:

➢ Describe the five philosophical approaches to teaching

➢ Describe one short example of a teaching practice for each approach

➢ Ask the participants to describe a practice-activity and representative approach

➢ Administer the Philosophy of Education Scale

➢ Ask participants to identify the highest and lowest scored approach

➢ Ask participants to list a practice or activity for the high and low approach

➢ Ask members to list the highest-lowest scored approaches for their entire group

➢ Ask members to organize a working plan to include the philosophical approaches that represent the entire group

Activity

You might have concerns, projects, or policies that are in conflict with some or all parents, teachers, or district principals. Do the questions above reveal philosophical approaches that were unknown to you? Should you hire a teacher with a different approach to balance the staffing of your school?

List your concerns or conflicts here.

Job Interviews

The Administrator

How to Conduct an Interview
The philosophical approaches of the administrator and applicant are important to the job interview process. As an applicant, you will have completed paperwork that contains a formal philosophy of education statement. The district human resources director and campus principal will read this statement and want to ask questions about the implications of your statement. These might be general or specific questions about teaching or related to a policy such your grading policy.

Sample Questions to Ask a Job Applicant:
As you ask these and other questions, list the words-phrases that represent the applicant's philosophical teaching approach.

1. Your teaching practices and activities represent your beliefs about teaching. Explain your beliefs and why you think they are important.

2. A good parental relationships can support student success in school Explain your approach to developing this relationship.

3. There are various approaches to grading. Describe your approach and how this approach supports student achievement.

4. What is your approach to homework? What is the basis for this approach?

5. If students learn in various styles, how do you approach teaching to accommodate these styles?

6. Describe your approach to curriculum development. How does this approach influence the strategies you implement in written lesson plans?

7. Your classroom environment reflects your philosophical beliefs about how students learn best. Describe your approach to classroom environment.

8. How will you approach classroom management? What philosophy of education best describes this approach and what are the benefits of this approach?

9. As a teacher leader, your role in the community is important. Describe your role as a teacher?

10. What is the most important goal of education today?

Activity: In mock interviews, practice asking these questions and noting the word-phrase responses of applicants.

The Job Applicant

How to Respond to an Administrator's Questions

An administrator will want to know that you have a clear definition of your philosophy of education and that you can explain how you will implement this philosophy in the classroom. If you are a candidate for a non-teaching position, such as a curriculum director, or assistant principal, these questions are also commonly asked of applicants.

You might have more than one interview and will need to respond to questions by any of the following district personnel: district human resources administrator, campus grade level team, or department chair, or campus principal, or district superintendent.

Applicants often ask if they should change their philosophy of education in order to get hired. This is a reasonable question that should be explored before you interview. In most cases, a district needs to hire staff that reflects the breadth of philosophical approaches. This broad staffing brings needed insight into solving school issues. In some cases, a principal might have three executive teachers and want to hire a more humanist teacher—as balance to the department or grade level. A school might have a parent who believes their child needs a more individualized approach to learning with less executive tasks. Or, a principal might want to employ a teacher whose philosophical approach is balanced in two areas, such as: subject-specialist *and* citizen teacher.

Sample Questions and Responses

One method for preparing for a job interview is to develop a set of responses to topic areas such as homework, and use your philosophical approach to discuss each topic. Using this strategy, all responses will reflect your main philosophical approach, as well as a secondary less frequently used approach. A second strategy is to review the questions on the previous page, and develop responses to each question, highlighting your two most favored philosophical approaches. The benefit of the second strategy is the flexibility offered; you will be able to respond to questions by described two approaches you most favor.

Respond to These Sample Questions

List the words-phrases that represent your philosophical teaching approach.

➢ **Sample Question**
Your teaching practices and activities represent your beliefs about teaching. Describe these and why you think they are important to teaching and learning

Sample Response: Humanist

I believe that learning takes place best when students are given a choice of how to learn and have a chance to try out materials that they like to use. I am a student centered teacher and I try to foster student interest in a subject. I do this by using mathematics manipulatives in small group activities.

How would you answer this question?
Write your answer here.

> ## Sample Question

Positive teacher-parent relationships can support student success in school Explain your approach to developing this relationship.

Sample Response: Citizen Teacher

Students should learn about their community and see their parents involved in school activities. This approach ties a community together. I ask students to invite their parents to campus for Friday lunch. Here, students learn about some of the Parents they have not met and their work, and parents learn about some of the student's abilities in reading. Some parents stay on as reading tutors.

How would you answer this question?
Write your answer here.

➢ Sample Question

There are various approaches to grading.
Describe your approach and how this approach supports student achievement.

Sample Response: Explorer

I communicate with my students on-line almost everyday. I like this approach because they are always searching for new information. When I grade their work, I already know how they used various resources. I post an on-line rubric for them to evaluate their searches. This is part of how I grade their work.

> How would you answer this question?
> Write your answer here.

➢ Sample Question

What is your approach to homework? What is the basis for this approach?

Sample Response: Subject Specialist

I spend time after school and on weekends reading and visiting museums.
I expect that my students will be involved in learning from various sources.
I give them open-ended assignments that they can use to meet broad curriculum goals. Many of them think up their own homework and reports. They are curious about the books I read and I even offer these for their homework.

> How would you answer this question?
> Write your answer here.

> ## Sample Question
If students learn in various styles, how do you approach teaching to accommodate these styles?

Sample Response: Humanist
I believe the teacher should help each student become the best person they can. This means that I have to look for all kinds of materials and approaches. Some students learn best with hand-on material, others in independent activities. There is no one-way to teach all children

How would you answer this question?
Write your answer here.

> ## Sample Question.
Describe your approach to curriculum development.
How does this approach influence the strategies you use in written lesson plans?

Sample Response: Executive
Student achievement is dependent upon clear learning objectives. I follow the guidelines in national and state standards and organize my lesson plans around these objectives. If a student misses class, I make certain they have the material so they can reach the objective. I have organized a yearlong curriculum that follows standards and helps all students achieve.

How would you answer this question?
Write your answer here.

> **Sample Question.**
> Your classroom environment reflects your philosophical beliefs about how students learn best. Describe this environment and your approach to this arrangement

Sample Response: Explorer

My classroom is arranged so that students can access technology and work together on projects. I use small centers to organize these groups. Students are free to move among the groups, seeking information that fits their project. Sometimes, students re-arrange the classroom environment because the group size and use of computers, or scanners does not work. They re-configure the environment and are inventive.

How would you answer this question?
Write your answer here.

> **Sample Question**
> How will you approach classroom management?
> What philosophy of education describes your approach and what benefit is this approach to students' learning?

Sample Response: Citizen Teacher

In my classroom, a participatory approach to management is used. The class and I develop a type of town hall or class meeting—like a class circle. Here we develop a list of classroom behaviors and expectations. These are like the laws of a community. Students learn that a citizen in a classroom and in a community is responsible for to the law of that community. They develop communication skills.

How would you answer this question?
Write your answer here.

➤ Sample Question
As a teacher leader, your role in the community is important.
Describe your role as a teacher.

Sample Response: Humanist
The role of a teacher is to bring together all possible support constituencies for the success of a student. This might mean that I wear different hats. I visit the homes of my students; sometimes, their parents come to visit me. None of my students are unknown to me and they know that I care about them and their families. The teacher is an important part of their life.

How would you answer this question?
Write your answer here.

➤ Sample Question
What is the most important goal of education today?

Response: Executive
The most important goal of education today is student attainment. The future of our country rests on the abilities of its citizens. Students must become good readers and communicators. They must have the ability to write effectively and use mathematics computation and scientific inquiry in the process of learning. Development of these skills will ensure their future success, and that of society at large.

How would you answer this question?
Write your answer here

NOTES

Practice Interview Sessions

Interviewing Techniques

> ➢ Respond to questions using four to six sentences.
> Do not add to this response unless asked by the interviewer to explain

> ➢ Use the four-sentence rule for explanations. If asked to explain if you have
> changed your philosophical approach to teaching explain in 4 sentences only.

Activity #1:   Peer Mock Interviews.
Practice responding to questions.
List important word-phrase responses of each participant.

Activity #2 Group Mock Interviews.
In small groups of four to six individuals, practice responding to questions.
List important word-phrase responses of each participant.
Compare these responses to your own word-phrases.
Make a list of word-phrases you like best.

Graduate School Applications

The purpose of writing a philosophy of education statement for application to graduate school is to convey to the reader a sense of the writer's background and future goals. An applicant should be able to describe their philosophical approach to teaching and learning, their experiences in applying this philosophy and the potential areas in which they believe they can impact education. A philosophy statement written for graduate school applications are usually one to two pages in length.

What are the main points to include?

➢ **Use this six-point paragraph format**

      o One paragraph describing the type of community and schooling you experienced in grades K-12.

      o One paragraph describing the goal of education

      o One paragraph describing the role of the teacher

      o One paragraph describing sample activities that indicates your philosophical approach to teaching

      o One paragraph describing your approach to classroom environment, management and grading-evaluation

      o One paragraph describing your personal and professional goals as a teacher

➢ Adjust the writing tense of each paragraphs to accommodate current employment

➢ Do not dwell on biographical information ("raised in a small town", or "married with three children"). This should be a brief introductory paragraph.

➢ Link your work experience to your future goals.

Example:
"My first degree is in psychology, which I used in business. For this work, I learned record keeping and several software programs. My future goals include learning how to develop large databases for future employment as a district research director. I plan to enroll in computer, statistics, and mathematics courses. I will also take coursework in testing and measurement, curriculum development and program evaluation. I believe documenting student achievement is a critical district need".

Using Your Philosophy Statement in a University Interview

Interviews for admittance to university graduate school programs are often conducted with small groups of faculty subject specialists. If you are interviewing to receive a fellowship or assistantship from the university, you might also be asked to write a philosophy of education statement and to present this philosophy to a group of faculty.

➤ Begin your interview with a brief philosophical statement.

➤ Use the six-sentence rule for statements of belief. Respond to questions using four to six sentences. Do not add to this response unless asked by the interviewer to explain.

➤ Use the four-sentence rule for explanations of statements. If asked to explain if you have changed your philosophical approach to teaching after a number of years as a teacher, explain in four sentences only. Expand again only if asked.

Activity #1: Peer Mock Interviews.
Practice responding to questions.
List important word-phrase responses of each participant

Activity #2 Group Mock Interviews.
In groups of four to six, practice responding to interview questions.
List important word-phrase responses of each participant.
Compare these responses to your own word-phrases.

Staff Development Leadership

Identify Participants' Philosophical Approach

> Describe the five philosophical approaches to teaching

> Describe one short example of a teaching practice for each approach

> Ask the participants to describe a practice-activity and representative approach

> Administer the Philosophy of Education Scale

> Ask participants to identify the highest and lowest scored approach

> Ask participants to list a practice or activity for the high and low approach

> Ask members to list the highest-lowest scored approaches for their entire group

Develop Group Goals that Everyone Likes!

> Ask members to organize a working plan to include the philosophical approaches that represents the entire group

> Ask members to develop a list of strategies and practices that represents the philosophies of the entire group

Invent a Common Vision

> Remember your district mission statement. Be certain all participants understand the long-range district goals.

> Remind participants that a mission statement is a vision—a philosophy statement is the perception of how to "get there" beliefs about how best to implement the mission

> If you are working with several groups (third and fourth grade level teams) Plan for each group to present philosophical approaches and indicators of practices and activities for each approach.

> Invent a common vision of best philosophical approaches for school-wide practice. Be certain that grade level, content area and teachers' philosophy are represented.

Appendices

- *Appendix A*
  Historical Aspects of Five Philosophical Approaches to Teaching

- *Appendix B*
  Table of Philosophic Ideas

- *Appendix C*
  Philosophy Web Sites

Appendix A
Historical Aspects of Philosophical Approaches

The Executive Approach

The executive approach to teaching is an orientation or framework that understands social practice and institutions (such as education) by the way they serve the survival of the social system (Feinberg & Soltis, 1998; Wactler, 1990). In the case of American education, the social system is served by the belief in the inherent right of all people to be well educated. Thomas Jefferson, for example, drew his justification for mass education from the notion of social fairness and the need for citizens to be educated for participation in the democratic process. To create this educated populace, schools communicate a belief in the role and responsibilities of an individual in a social order.

Long before American authors wrote in support of the independent and executive role of the learner in schools, historical figures, such as Aristotle proposed this same learner role. Aristotle incorporated the ideal of empirical observation into his view of truth and knowledge and incorporated teaching techniques such as lectures and classic writing (Smith, 1984). Aristotle argued that difference among people could be mediated by the interaction of nature suggesting the use of schools for scientific exploration and achievement. This direct-learning approach to teaching and learning formed early 20th century education educational philosophies.

In an attempt to educate large numbers of students in early 20th century public schools, an efficiency model was developed. Here, one teacher was placed with a classroom of children of the same chronological age. This efficiency formula for teaching is similar to a business model that attempts to do more for less effort. The focus of learning in the executive model is the transfer of knowledge from one source (teacher, textbook, computer program) to the learner. Here, the measurement of success in education is the quantity of knowledge transferred, particularly if fewer resources (e.g., fewer teachers) are needed to transfer this knowledge. Twentieth century psychologists who advocated for programmed instruction in schools supported this philosophical approach.

Behaviorism as described by psychologist B.F. Skinner (1968) is based on the belief that learning is the observable outcome of a stimulus-response experience that is incrementally reinforced (Richelle, 1993). Skinner's work with laboratory animals suggested to behaviorists that learning is controllable and can be increased if the optimal reinforcement schedule is maintained. American schools began adoption of several behavioristic activities such as programmed instructional materials, reward systems, such as grading systems, and reward-punishment contingencies.

Current research regarding approaches to teaching has found aspects of behavioristic-executive approaches an effective philosophy. Berliner (1983) and Hunter (1971) noted that the way in which teachers structure the learning environment and instructional tasks, does, in fact, impact learning. Thus, the executive approach is often advocated as a *traditional* approach to teaching. Additional behavioristic-executive historical figures and perspectives are found in Appendix B.

The Humanist Approach

The central focus of the humanist approach to teaching is consideration of the needs and abilities of each individual. Research on this approach has emphasized the significant role of the learner in his or her own learning (Chomsky, 1959; Tanner & Tanner, 1995). A teacher using this approach develops cognitive learning strategies that activates an individual's prior knowledge (Pinar & Grumet, 1976; Pinar, 1989) and includes the context in which learning takes place (Eisner, 1982; Giddens, 1984; McCarthy-Tucker & Pryor, 2000) Anthropologists such as Margaret Mead (1951) charged American educators to study the changing contexts of students' socialization and upbringing in order to become better teachers (Bogdan & Bicklen, 1982). Use of students' prior knowledge and social context to enhance learning was popularized in the work of psychologists such as Carl Rogers (1969; 1980) and Abraham Maslow (1970). Maslow encouraged educators to consider students' needs in their development of school curriculum. A model of Maslow's 1970 hierarchy of needs is shown here.

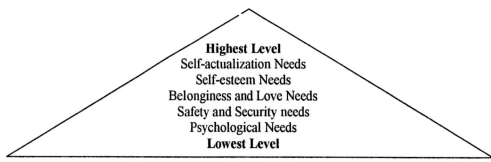

Highest Level
Self-actualization Needs
Self-esteem Needs
Belonginess and Love Needs
Safety and Security needs
Psychological Needs
Lowest Level

During the 18th century, the humanist approach proved a challenge to established society. The humanist proposition of the importance of self-efficacy and individual right to creative choice came in conflict with established social class organization, government and religious doctrines (Smith, 1984). Educators such as Pestalozzi and Froebel however, encouraged the idea that individuals should be able to control their own destiny and through their expression of individual perspective. In 1799, Pestalozzi developed a children's village, a school known as the cradle of today's elementary school (Downs, 1975). By 1811, Froebel had come in contact with Pestalozzi and began his own school—the Child's Nurture and Activity Institute. Froebel's Institute was later termed the Kindergarten –a place for children to develop as *small flowers* (Lawrence, 1953). Froebel published play materials and songs for children; the Italian physician, Maria Montessori and American kindergarten educator, Susan Blow, adapted his methods.

Twentieth century adaptations of the humanist approach to teaching can be seen in the work of John Dewey. Dewey wrote in support of an individual's need to learn through discovery and inquiry (1913; 1933; 1964). Dewey's believed in the education of the whole child by suggestion that is an education should be practical and adaptable to real work of society. Methods encouraged by Dewey focused on the use of a scientific-discovery method, a hands-on-type of learning using of manipulative materials. Dewey encouraged teachers to use group interaction and socialization to help students to learn about cooperation, responsibility and community effort. Dewey's suggestion for educators to encourage cooperation is currently used in classroom strategies such as the cooperative learning model of Johnson & Johnson (1984).

The *Subject Specialist* Approach

Educational models from the early Greek period (399 B.C.) are the basis of the subject specialist approach to teaching. Socrates is noted for utilizing a didactic method of teaching. Here, the teacher question students and uses rhetoric (higher order thinking questions) in their manner of reply to students. The subject specialist approach is also termed a *liberationist* or *classicist* approach as subject areas content is central to the approach (Fenstermacher & Soltis, 1998). This approach has critiques as socially hierarchical because particular types of knowledge and subjects are rated for social desirability. However, the approach assumes a "love of learning" in which the precedent for curricular inclusion is the rigor of the subject (Smith, 1984).

In the pre-Christian era of the Greek experience, the emphasis on learning included individual commitment to judicious skepticism and inquiry. Socrates modeled such skepticism by teaching his students to use questioning and inquiry as part or argument (Smith, 1984). Following Socrates, Plato and Aristotle formalized this process by developing academies that set forth high standards for demonstrating knowledge of a subject and personal independence of scholarship (Smith, 1984).

An example of the Greek model of education derived from Aristotelian logic of the 13th century is scholasticism. Here, the teacher and the students each state a problem and then list arguments for and against a solution to the problem. In order to demonstrate knowledge of a subject, the speaker is required to use rational and logical analysis of each solution. Brevity and clarity are virtues of scholasticism (Smith, 1984). St. It has been said that Thomas Aquinas perfected scholasticism as he embodied the convictions of Christian theology in teaching in a manner that emphasized the need for human reasoning as a determinant of truth (Smith, 1984).

A number of 20th century educators have embraced the perspectives of the subject specialist approach. Mortimer Adler and Robert Hutchins professors and co-editors of the Encyclopedia Britannica were philosophically committed to the importance of subject knowledge in the educational curriculum. The ability to use one's mind for practice—thus the analogy that the "mind is a muscle" is important to the perspective of the subject specialist. This approach assumes that practice in higher order thinking is exercise for the mind and results in the ability to think and reason well. Hutchins and Adler advocated the use of a classic reading program they developed, *The Great Books of the Western World*, as the basis for school curriculum development. This program was used in eth period from 1930 to the early 1960's. By the mid-1960's, thematic-integrated education programs (combining math and science, or reading and social studies) such as those proposed by James B. Conant became more common, and the basis of preparation for thousands of high school students. The progressive movement of humanism again became attractive in curriculum development in the late 1970's (Ravitch, 1984).

The subject specialist philosophical approach has current adherents that use two sub-philosophical approaches. The first approach is termed *essentialist*, an approach that suggests a particular body of knowledge, taught in a manner that depicts the design of the knowledge, is essential for all educated individuals (Fenstermacher & Soltis, 1998). An example of essential knowledge is asking students to recite the multiplication tables *and describe* the mathematics process. The second approach of a subject specialist is a *perennialist approach*. The perennialist believes that knowledge will free man's mind and enhance their understanding of the constraints upon their life. Here, the goal of education is freedom and independent thinking (Freire, 1970; Fenstermacher & Soltis, 1998 and Feinberg & Soltis, 1998).

The Citizen Teacher Approach

The principles regarding citizenship, particularly those of democratic citizenship are derived from the Greek thought in the 300 B.C. period in and adapted during in the American colonial period (Smith, 1984). Three of these principles are: liberty and freedom, justice and fairness, and equality and equal opportunity (Ravitch, 1984; Parker, 1996) and their use as a basis for teacher leadership constitutes a *citizen teacher* philosophical approach to teaching.

Early 20th century theorists, such as John Dewey, proposed that educators center their educational practice on the principle of liberty by engaging students in discovery through self-directed learning. Dewey believed in the importance of creating a learning environment that encouraged each student to think independently, implement their own ideas and consider the needs of others. These experiences, Dewey wrote, would enhance the civic ability of students whose decisions would become central to decisions for the good of a democracy (1933).

Implementing teaching strategies to promote students' independence of thought--freedom of thought, however was an entirely new philosophical approach in 20th century teaching practice. Common practice in this period were methods such as recitation and memory, activities designed to elicit common responses from an entire group of students (Smith, 1984). Often, students could be heard chanting and reciting poetry or bible passages with educational success dependent on the perfection of these skills. Few teachers were trained to implement a curriculum that highly engaged students' independent thinking, creative abilities, or interests in life-long learning and employment (Oliva, 2001).

Progressive education appeared to meet this need, as it centered on humanistic concerns. Dewey and others involved in educational reform of this era, however insisted that preparation for participation in the responsibilities of citizenship called for a more overt, practical curriculum. Devey argued that the work of school should be linked to work found in society. He proposed that classrooms that evidenced democratic ideals (democratic practice) helped children understand democratic ideas. This reform of the *progressive education era* necessitated the development of courses such as "life-long living" or "health education" in order to prepare students for their life's work (Tanner & Tanner, 2001). Thus, the influence of progressive-humanists perspectives is evident in the citizen teacher approach, but the approach differs from humanism as the goal of the citizen teacher is to develop an understanding of the history and practice of democratic ideas. This difference is evident in the manner in which teachers develop curriculum.

Using student interests (humanism) in a democratic (fair and just) manner required that schools provide for equal opportunity among all learners (citizens). One example of the citizen teacher approach is the consideration given to classroom organization. Although individual exploration of content information with "hands-on or self-generated activities" is encouraged in the classroom environment, the citizen teacher, not unlike the Greeks before them, expect that students can find practical outcomes for their exploration and generate well reasoned arguments that serve the good of the classroom community. One example of student-directed classrooms is the notable popularity of schools organized by Maria Montessori (1870-1952) who envisioned the role of the teacher was to facilitate student exploration and inquiry (Smith, 1984). Democratic education remained popular during the periods of 1903-1940, and in part during the 1970's.

The mid- 1980's ushered in an era—present today—of teaching to common measurable objectives and administration of standardized tests with teacher accountability for test results. Democratic education, however, was not without adherents to teaching a common knowledge core. Around the early 1990's some curriculum theorists suggested that common core knowledge (e.g., mathematics, social studies, science) could be enhanced by a *parallel* pedagogy --the integration of democratic principles into classroom practices (e.g., Tanner & Tanner, 1995; Oliva, 2001). Not all policy makers agree with the suggestion for pedagogical integration of democratic practices; rather, they argue that the three principles of democratic thought should be implemented as a "stand alone" approach in which teaching about democracy is a *separate* core content area of the curriculum (e.g., Gutmann, 1987). Currently, integrating democratic principles into a standards-based core curriculum appears to have prevailed. Teachers remain committed to teaching the state mandated content standards, however, interest in modifications of instructional decisions to include democratic principles remains high (Pryor, 2003).

The *Explorer* Approach

The explorer approach blends elements of the content-based subject specialist approach with aspects of the humanists approach. Teachers using this approach often employ strategies that appear humanist (e.g., group work or peer coaching). However, the philosophical goal of the explorer approach is *not* self-actualization. The goal of education in this approach is to determine truth, make sense of information, and re-construct values within a society. The role of the teacher as explorer is to assist students to develop and filter social values through which they determine the importance of information and the possibilities for use of information. As a teaching style, the explorer teacher often appears as an assistant, working in a parallel manner with students. At times, the role of teacher and student are reversed, as the teacher might about the use of technology or information from their students.

Theoretically, the explorer approach to teaching can be contrasted with more traditional or executive approaches to teaching. For example, the notion of the use of time in school has had an executive history. Patrick Slattery (1995) noted that in the executive approach, time is perceived as linear, hierarchical and quantifiable (p.3). Executive teachers often measure and evaluate students for efficient use of time Students might be asked, "Have you finished yet"? or "Did you turn your work in on time"? In order to determine if a student is competent, they might ask, "Who finished first"?

In contrast, the explorer approach to teaching is based on existentialism, a perspective that meaning is derived from the individual's sense of what is real. Philosophers such as Jean-Paul Sartre (1905-1980) used the term *existentialism* in 1947 to represent a "renewed interest on existing things" (Cantalano, 1996, p. 578). Sartre's pointedly infused the structure of things (not necessarily objects) with the presence [interpretation] given to a thing by human activity. In the case of sense making, an individual is taught to de-structure [take-apart] and then re-construct information. In the case of self, individuals are taught to recreate a sense of self through life, experience and knowledge. The term *existentialism* refers to the teaching approach in which a teacher provides the opportunity for individuals to make sense of their own learning (Cantalano, 1996; Fenstermacher & Soltis, 1998; Wactler, 1990).

The complexity of *making sense of information* often challenges teachers to create environments in which vast amounts of information can become accessible. This deconstruction of school curriculum models is termed *post-modernism*, and reflection on and reorganization of schools models is termed *reconstructionism*, both sub-philosophical perspectives of existentialism (Slattery, 1995). Slattery wrote that the school curriculum should be thought of as flexible and time should be viewed as a resource whose importance is on how it is used rather than if it is used efficiently (1995).

Doll (1993) has suggested that the existentialist (explorer) philosophy calls for a shift in curriculum and in how learners view their role. This shift in learner role suggests that teachers think of student learning in an active rather than passive perspective, with knowledge in a transitory or incomplete state (Doll, 1993).

Appendix B

TABLE OF PHILOSOPHIC IDEAS

INDIVIDUAL	DATE	CONCEPTS
Thucydides Athens, Greece	440-400 B. C.	Power to govern belongs to all people. People are equal under the law. Wrote *The Peloponnesian War* as a metaphor for the values of democracy. The hero, Pericles, defends the rule of law and extends freedom to all people.
Plato Athens, Greece	428-347 B.C.	Individuals descend from self-interest to communal need. Result may be a shift in focus of democracy. Emphasis: Individual Freedom.
Aristotle Athens, Greece	384-322 B.C.	Preference of Polity (democracy with elements of oligarchy and moderation); however, Athens introduced notions of personal freedom, rule of law, and importance of a large middle class. Emphasis: Numeric equality, majority rules. People are free when they can live as they like.
John Locke England	1632-1704	The consent of the governed as argument for freedom creates the case against a monarchy. A participatory body politic is necessary to continue a civil society. Faith (and opportunity) itself leads to free thinking.
John Stuart Mill England	1806-1873	Political liberty is so necessary that education should only be content bound (objective) education. The majority becomes the government. Freedom of thought and action lead to a steady improvement in the happiness of humankind.
Benjamin Franklin America	1706-1790	Independence (freedom) must be balanced by social needs without some form of government, despotic government (the end of freedom) could occur. Governments are not perfect but needed establishments, when well administered. Government secures freedom.
Thomas Jefferson America	1743-1826	Liberty is a natural human state. Given freedom of thought, each of his fellow human beings was thought of as capable of exercising powers as a citizen, intelligently and responsibly. A democratic state consists of a populace that is well educated.

(Pryor, 2002)

INDIVIDUAL	DATE	CONCEPTS
Protagoras Athens, Greece	c. 490-420 B.C.	If properly taught, a human being can demonstrate *virtue and intelligence in the governing process*. He/she can learn what is right and lawful and what is good and that we benefit from fair dealing.
Alcuin England	735-804	Part of the Carolingian Renaissance that encouraged schooling to children, including the children of serfs (workers), and improving knowledge through accuracy in language and books.
St. Thomas Aquinas Italy	c.1224-1274	A scholastic and Aristotelian thinker of the Christian church. Justification of *faith and reason* giving hope to the use of intellect for every man.
John Locke England	1632-1704	Espoused a practical liberalism and the justification of popular government and argued for *consent of the governed* as argument for a just society. Social integration requires the training of the full person.
Jean-Jacques Rousseau Switzerland	1712-1778	Society potentially manipulates the weak. Personal freedom(s) can be lost to social needs and personal freedom would remain a priori to social needs. Inference to *just and fair society* and case against monarchy.
Maria Montessori Italy	1870-1952	First female physician in Italy. Defined potential success of mental effort that can be considered *just and fair* (e.g., that "mental deficiency was more an educational than a medical problem" [Smith, 1984])."
John Dewey America	1859-1952	Exploration or discovery supports democratic practice. Activism in thinking about one's teaching (as is reflection) is empowerment. Experience arbitrates and encourages the self to create knowledge. Society is maintained (as in a just and fair society) by the independence of participants.

(Pryor, 2002)

INDIVIDUAL	DATE	CONCEPTS
Cicero Rome, Italy	106-43 B.C.	Supported equal distribution of land (conquered) and rights for peasants. Wrote *On Oratory* as appeal for wider and broader education (than rhetoric only) in order to promote "wisdom, patriotism, courage, Aristotelian temperance, moral goodness, and oratorical eloquence" (Smith, 1984).
Benedict Rome, Italy	480-c.543	Education should be (in his case, for monks) literate, for the people. Children also should learn beyond the basics of ABC's and be instructed in language, rhetoric, logic, and religion. Monasteries became an important economic and educational unit of their particular locality (Smith, 1984).
Mary Wollstonecraft England	1759-1797	Wrote *Vindication of the Rights of Woman*, an analysis of women's subservience. Proposed an egalitarian alternative to inequalities in British society. Proposed that pedagogy "served to empower or disenfranchise particular social groups." Espoused the ability to think rationally as a skill vital to success (Smith, 1984).
Thomas Paine America	1737-1809	An individual's ability to reason must be promoted. Social inventions derive from social constructs (constraining).
William Godwin America	1756-1836	Exercise of human reason rather than upholding a national Agenda promotes human beings. Feared that society may Engulf human beings.
John Stuart Mill America	1806-1873	The majority becomes the government. Political liberty is So necessary that education should only be content bound (objective education).
Paulo Freire Brazil	1921-1997	Wrote *Pedagogy of the Oppressed* (1970). Brought education to the poor and taught a dialectical method of learning. Created a consciousness for literacy as a means of empowerment. Interested adults in literacy for democracy.
Thomas Sowell America	Contemporary	Newspaper columnist. Promotes excellence in educational attainment as contributing to the strength of a nation, particularly the democratic endeavors of independence found in American government.
Amy Gutmann America	Contemporary	Education for democracy is essential. One's own ideas could result in repressive and discriminatory ideas. Lack of minority option is evidenced by lack of minority voice in social/political structure. All curricula can impose a value position and the human mind cannot be freed by objectification.

(Pryor, 2002)

Appendix C
Philosophy Websites

www.ncss.org National Council of the Social Studies

mhhe.com/socscience/education/spring Joel Spring website

http://cuip.net/pes/ or new web page: http://www.ed.uiuc.edu/eps/pes/
Philosophy of Education Society, University of Illinois

http://cuip.net/pes/intres.htm Philosophy of Education Internet Resources

http://cuip.net/pes/pubs.htm Philosophy of Education Society Publications

http://www.ed.uiuc.edu/EPS/Educational-Theory/
> EDUCATIONAL THEORY (ISSN 0013-2004) publishes work in the philosophy of
> education and other disciplines. It is co-sponsored by the John Dewey Society, the Philosophy of Education
> Society, the College of Education at the University of Illinois at Urbana-Champaign and the College of
> Education at the University of Illinois at Chicago.

http://cuip.net/pes/listserv.htm Philosophy of Education List serve

http://www.bu.edu/wcp/MainEduc.htm Philosophy of Education Archived Papers

http://www.kluweronline.com/issn/0039-3746 Journal: Studies in Philosophy and Education

http://www.molloy.edu/academic/philosophy/sophia/TOPICS/education.htm
> Classical resources in philosophy of education

http://www.ilt.columbia.edu/academic/spaces/philosophy/
> Teachers College, Columbia University, Study space in philosophy

http://www.vusst.hr/ENCYCLOPAEDIA/popper_and_the_philosophy_of_edu.htm
> Theoretical perspective on the nature of science

http://www.bc.edu/libraries/resources/guides/s-philoseduc/
> Research guide in philosophy of education: Boston College

References

Berliner, D. (1983). The executive functions of teaching. *Instructor, 9,* 29-39.

Bogdan, R., & Bicklen, S. (1982). *Qualitative research for education: An introduction to theory and methods.* Boston: Allyn & Bacon.

Catalano, J.S. (1996). Sartre. In (J.J. Chambliss, Ed.), *Philosophy of Education: An Encyclopedia,* 578-580. New York: Garland Publishing.

Chomsky, N. (1959). Review of Skinner's verbal behavior. *Language, 35,* 26-38.

Connell, W.F. (1980). *A History of Education in the Twentieth Century World.* Curriculum Development Centre: Canberra, Australia.

Dewey, J. (1910). *How we think.* New York: Heath.

Dewey, J. (1933). *A re-statement of the relation of reflective thinking to the educative process.* Lexington, MA: D. C. Heath.

Dewey, J. (1964). *Democracy in education.* New York: Mcmillan.

Doll Jr., W. (1993). *A post-modern perspective on curriculum.* New York: Teachers College Press.

Downs, R. (1975). *Heinrich Pestalozzi: Father of modern pedagogy.* New York: Twayne.

Eisner, E.W. (1982). *Cognition and curriculum. A basis for deciding what to teach.* New York: Longman.

Feinberg, W. & Soltis, J. (1998). *School and society.* New York: Teachers College Press.

Fenstermacher, G., & Soltis, J. (1998). *Approaches to teaching.* New York: Teachers College Press.

Freire, P. (1970). *Pedagogy of the oppressed.* (M. B. Ramso, Trans.). New York: Seabury Press.

Giddens, A. (1984). The constitution of society: Outline of the theory of structuration. Cambridge, England: Polity Press.

Gutmann, A. (1987). *Democratic education.* Princeton: Princeton University Press.

Hunter, M. (1971). *Teach for transfer.* El Segundo, CA: TIP Publications.

Hutchins, R. (1952). Great books of the western world. In (M. Adler & R. Hutchins, Eds.),

The New Encyclopedia Britannica. V 20, 24-26. Chicago: Encyclopedia Britannica.

Johnson, A. P. (2002). *A short guide to action research.* Boston: Allyn & Bacon.

Johnson, D., Johnson, R., Holubec, E., & Roy, P. (1984). *Circles of learning.* Alexandria, VA: Association for Supervision and Curriculum Development.

Lawrence, E. (1953). *Fredrich Froebel and English education.* New York: Philosophical Library, Inc.

Maslow, A. (1970). *Motivation and Personality.* (2nd ed.). New York. Philosophical Library, Inc.

Mead, M. (1951). *The school in American culture.* Cambridge, Mass.: Harvard University Press.

McCarthy-Tucker, S.N. & Pryor, C.R. (2000). Teaching style, philosophical orientation and the transmission of critical thinking skills in U.S. public schools. *The Korean Journal of Thinking and Problem Solving. 10*(1) 69-77.

Oliva, P. (2000). *Developing the curriculum.* (4th Ed.) New York: Harper & Row.

Parker, W. (1996). Curriculum for democracy. In R. Soder (Ed.), *Democracy, education and the schools (pp. 182-210).* San Francisco, CA: Jossey-Bass.

Pinar,W. F. (1989). A reconceptualization of teacher education. *Journal of Teacher Education. 40*(1). 9-12.

Pinar, W. F., & Grumet, M (1976). *Towards a poor curriculum.* Dubuque, IA: Kendall/Hunt.

Pryor, C. (2002). *Democratic practice workbook: Activities for the field experience.* Boston: McGraw-Hill.

Pryor, C.R. & Pryor, B.W. (November, 2003). *Preservice teachers' intentions to implement democratic practice: A longitudinal study of attitude and beliefs.* Paper presented to the College and University Faculty at the meeting of the National Council of the Social Studies.

Publication Manual of the American Psychological Association (5th ed.). (2001). Washington, DC: American Psychological Association.

Ravitch, D. (1984). *The troubled crusade: American education 1945-1980.*

Richelle, M. (1993). *B. F. Skinner: A Reappraisal.* Hove (UK): Lawrence Erlbaum Associates, 171-172.

Rogers, C. (1969). *Freedom to learn.* Columbus, Ohio: Charles E. Merrill.

Rogers, C. (1980). *A way of being.* New York: Houghton Mifflin.

Skinner, B. F. (1968). *The technology of teaching.* New York: Appleton-Century-Crofts.

Slattery, P. (1995). *Curriculum development in the postmodern era.* New York: Garland.

Smith, M. (1984). *Lives in education.* Iowa State University Press.

Tanner, D., & Tanner, L. (1995). *Curriculum development.* New Jersey: Prentice Hall.

Tyler, R.W. (1949). *Basic principles of curriculum and instruction.* Chicago: University of Chicago Press.

Wactler, C.R. (1990). How student teachers make sense of student teaching: The derivations of an individual's educational philosophy. (Doctoral dissertation, Arizona State University, 1990).

Dissertation Abstracts International 51, 2627.

Wolcott, H. F. (2001). *Writing Up Qualitative Research.* Thousand Oaks, CA: Sage.

About the Author

Caroline R. Pryor is Assistant Professor of Social Studies Education and Regents Fellow at Texas A&M University, College Station, and 2003 Wye Fellow of the Aspen Institute and American Colleges and Universities. She holds a Bachelor of Arts degree in Anthropology from California State University, Northridge, a Masters in Higher and Adult Education and Doctorate in Secondary Education from Arizona State University, Tempe. Dr. Pryor also holds a lifetime teaching credential, grades K-9 and community college teaching certification.

Dr. Pryor has received numerous awards for teaching and research, including the *Best Paper Award* from the Arizona Educational Research Organization, state affiliate of American Educational Research Association. Her journal articles regard philosophy of education and democratic practices. Pryor's books include: *Philosophy of Education Workbook: Writing a Statement of Beliefs and Practices, Democratic Classroom Practice: Activities for the Field Experience, The Mission of the Scholar: Research and Practices,* and the forthcoming book, *Influencing Attitude and Behavior: A School Leader's Guide (with co-author B.W. Pryor).*

Dr. Pryor served as a member of the Association of Teacher Educators' Commission on Democratic Practice and the Commission on Affective Education, the Arizona State Department of Education's Commission on Citizenship Standards in Adult Education, and is currently serving on the committee on Citizenship for the College and University Faculty Assembly of the National Council of the Social Studies. Pryor is the current program chair of the Constructivism Research, Theory and Practice Special Interest Group of the American Educational Research Association.

Additional scales to measure philosophical perspectives of teaching or intentions to integrate democratic classroom practices can be found on Dr. Pryor's website:
http://tlac.coe.tamu.edu/faculty/facpages/pryor.html